Wonderful You!

To Josh:

I love you more.

We're definitely in this together.

Contents

Introduction

Here's a simple fact: You are wonderful! You are the only person on Earth with your exact strengths and gifts. You have everything you need inside of you to create an inspiring, fun, powerful life—right now.

Sometimes, we just need a reminder or a friend to pick us up, turn us around, and point out that we are valuable and capable beyond measure.

This book is that reminder. I have my master's degree in positive psychology, the science of happiness and human flourishing, and here is what we know from renowned researchers: Happiness is a choice. We don't choose what happens to us, but we can choose how we respond. We get to choose where we put our energy, what we think about, and what actions we take. We choose to let a situation take us down the drain or to shift gears and rise up as resilient, empowered, and purposeful.

I'm not saying that choosing happiness is easy—but it is possible. Laughter helps. Inspiration helps. Friendship helps. And that's what I hope to provide for you.

I've curated uplifting, encouraging, and sometimes quirky quotes on the basis of qualities that help people flourish: gratitude, confidence, resilience, positive mindset, and joy. Plus, I've included "Fun Facts" that teach you how to use the science of happiness to flourish!

I wrote this book because, like you, I need it. Even though I'm a happiness coach and motivational speaker, I've also lived with anxiety my whole life. As the youngest of three, I grew up desperate to be perfect. Perfect grades, perfect college, perfect marriage, and perfect house.

But I felt trapped in my perfect life, so I got divorced and went on a quest to understand what happiness was to me. Happiness comes down to two words: We CHOOSE. We're in charge of our own happiness. When we engage in activities we love, surround ourselves with nourishing relationships, do work that fulfills us, and rise up from challenges with courage, we feel wonderful.

When life gives you sh*t, turn it into fertilizer that sprouts your biggest dreams. When life controls you, hit PAUSE, breathe, and chart your own path forward. When you're stuck in negativity, pick up this book, get some positivity, and shift.

Ten years ago, I was robbed at gunpoint, and I promised myself that if I lived, I would pursue my purpose of inspiring and empowering others. And here I am today. I still get anxious and I still have challenges and traumas, but I remember to choose my path.

So, welcome, friend, to *Wonderful You!* Remember: You are strong. You are courageous. You are fabulous.

YOU ARE WONDERFUL!

You Are Magnif-icent!

YOU ARE ALLOWED TO BE BOTH A MASTER PIECE and A WORK IN PROGRESS, SIMULTANEOUSLY.

—SOPHIA BUSH

DON'T LET SOMEONE DIM *your* LIGHT SIMPLY BECAUSE IT'S *Shining* IN THEIR EYES

Wake up:
YOU'RE A
F*CKING
Miracle
OF
BEING

—GARY JOHN BISHOP

IF YOU CAN DANCE AND BE FREE AND NOT EMBARRASSED, YOU CAN RULE THE WORLD.

—AMY POEHLER

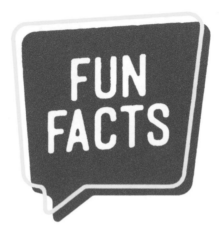

According to Harvard-trained physician and behavior change therapist Dr. Ali Binazir, your being alive is a one in 500 quadrillion chance. The odds of that sperm meeting that egg for your procreation are astronomically low, so don't waste this miraculous life by acting like someone else.

BEING *Original* DOESN'T REQUIRE

BEING FIRST

IT JUST MEANS BEING

DIFFERENT

& BETTER

—ADAM GRANT, PHD

DON'T BE LIKE the REST OF THEM DarLing.

—COCO CHANEL

Find Out Who You are and do it on Purpose

—DOLLY PARTON

WHAT SETS YOU
APART
CAN SOMETIMES FEEL LIKE
A BURDEN **&** IT'S NOT
AND A LOT OF TIME
IT'S WHAT MAKES YOU
GREAT

—EMMA STONE

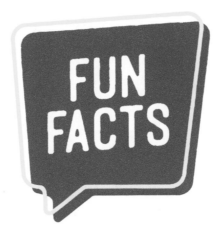

If Lucille Ball, Robin Williams, or Jim Carrey had hidden their uniqueness, we'd never have experienced their brilliance. So although you may think you should work on improving your weaknesses, doing so makes you more negative, grumpier, and achieve less every day. Instead, research shows that you should focus on your strengths, and you'll be more confident, more successful, and happier. Build on your strengths and soar!

WHY THE F*CK NOT ME?

should be your motto

—MINDY KALING

IF THEY DON'T GIVE you a SEAT at the TABLE, BRING a FOLDING CHAIR

—MAYA ANGELOU

I'M NOT a

PRINCESS,

I DON'T NEED

SAVING.

I'M a

QUEEN

I've got this sh*t

HANDLED.

—UNKNOWN

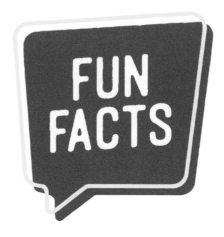

Instead of saying, "I'm awesome," say, "I can do this no matter what." The most successful people don't just have self-esteem—they have self-efficacy, the belief that given your strengths and abilities you can overcome any challenge and thrive. Be self-efficacious, my friend, and you will thrive.

Fierce Has many faces, and one of them is yours. **Perfect** is **boring**, **HUMAN** is **BEAUTIFUL**.

IF YOU COULD SEE YOURSELF JUST FOR ONE DAY YOU'D SEE HOW EVERYONE ELSE SEES YOU. AND MY GOD,

YOU ARE F*CKING BEAUTIFUL.

—UNKNOWN

ALWAYS REMEMBER,
YOU ARE THE SUNSHINE
TO THOSE WHO LOOK UP
TO YOU, AND THEY ARE YOUR
SUNBATHERS.
...SO GLOW BRIGHTLY, BE THAT
POSITIVE ENLIGHTENMENT
THAT RADIATES JOY INTO THEIR HEARTS
AND FILLS THEM WITH WARMTH AND POSITIVITY.
SO THAT THEY MAY DO THE SAME ONE DAY,
UNTO ALL THOSE SUNBATHERS WHO LOOK UP TO THEM.

—BODHI SMITH

THROUGH
YOUR OWN
TRANSFORMATION
AND EMBRACING YOUR
MAGNIFICENCE
YOU WILL AFFECT OTHERS
IN WAYS YOU MAY NEVER FULLY UNDERSTAND.
THIS IS WHAT CHANGES THE COURSE OF LIFE.
YES, YOU ARE THAT
POWERFUL

—FABIENNE FREDRICKSON

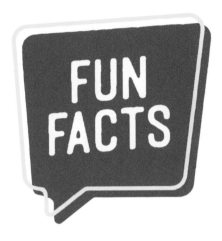

Our emotions are contagious up to three degrees of separation, so how awesome you feel rubs off on the barista at the coffee shop, your mail-delivery person, your kids, your co-workers, your neighbors, and the customer service agent you're forced to talk to when your electricity goes out. So choose to feel awesome, and let others benefit from your magnificence.

"YOU ChANGED"

IS A COMPLIMENT.

—RACHEL HOLLIS

THERE IS *Truth* INSIDE OF YOU

THAT HAS BEEN WAITING FOR YOU TO

DISCOVER

AND THE TRUTH IS THAT

YOU DESERVE

all good things life has to offer.

—RHONDA BYRNE

You're GOING to HAVE To LEARN to Pat yourself ON THE BACK EVENTUALLY. StarT NOW. IT'S NOT GLOATING. IT'S TAKING PLEASURE IN LIFE'S GOODNESS.

—PICABO STREET

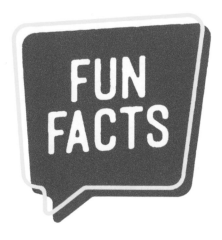

There's no other you, and you are here for your unique purpose! Researchers at the University of Illinois found that people with purpose have greater overall life satisfaction, even on crappy days. So listen to your heart, follow your truth, and celebrate yourself for taking the courageous path forward!

Little Things

I FINALLY FIGURED OUT the ONLY REASON TO BE ALIVE IS TO ENJOY IT

—RITA MAE BROWN

EACH ONE OF US has at our fingertips, access to so much MEANING & HOPE GOODNESS & BEAUTY in every moment if we would only LET OURSELVES SEE

You Only Live Once, BUT IF YOU DO IT RIGHT, Once Is ENOUGH.

—MAE WEST

WHAT YOU HAVE TO DECIDE... IS HOW YOU WANT YOUR LIFE TO BE. IF YOUR FOREVER WAS ENDING TOMORROW, WOULD THIS BE HOW YOU'D WANT TO HAVE SPENT IT? LISTEN, THE TRUTH IS, NOTHING IS GUARANTEED. YOU KNOW THAT MORE THAN ANYBODY. SO DON'T BE AFRAID. **BE ALIVE.**

—SARAH DESSEN

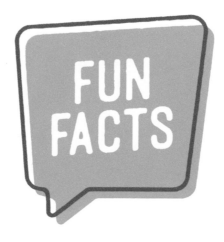

There are 1,440 minutes in a day and 8,760 hours in a year. Take at least a few of them to slow down, notice, and experience the little joyful things that lead to awesome happiness.

FRiENDSHiP IS ABOUT FINDING PEOPLE WHO are your KIND OF CRAZY

—UNKNOWN

Lots of people want to ride with you in the limo, but what you want is someone who will take the bus with you when the limo breaks down

—OPRAH WINFREY

Friends are like WALLS sometimes you lean on them, sometimes it's GOOD just knowing they're there.

—BERNARD MELTZER

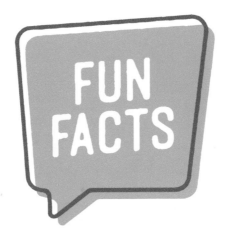

Having positive relationships has as much impact on your health as eating well, sleeping enough, and not smoking. We are social animals who get a hit of feel-good hormones when we even think about people we love. As a positive psychologist, Christopher Peterson, PhD, once said, "Other people matter," so call a friend today and fill up on joy.

SOMETIMES THE SMALLEST THINGS TAKE UP THE MOST ROOMS IN OUR HEARTS

—WINNIE THE POOH (BY A.A. MILNE)

Now and then it's good to **p a u s e**

in our pursuit of happiness **and** just **be happy**.

LIFE IS SHORT.

SMILE

WHILE YOU
HAVE TEETH.

—MALLORY HOPKINS

IT'S SO EASY TO WASTE OUR LIVES: OUR DAYS, OUR HOURS, OUR MINUTES. IT IS SO EASY TO TAKE FOR GRANTED THE PALE NEW GROWTH OF AN EVERGREEN, THE SHEEN OF LIMESTONE ON FIFTH AVENUE, THE COLOR OF OUR KIDS' EYES, THE WAY THE MELODY IN A SYMPHONY RISES AND FALLS AND DISAPPEARS AND RISES AGAIN. IT'S SO EASY TO EXIST INSTEAD OF LIVE.

—ANNA QUINDLEN

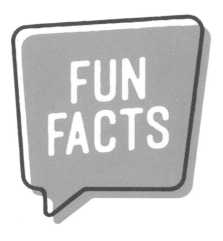

Quickly moving from one thing to the next causes stress and reduces our well-being. Savoring what's good ignites your brain's frontal lobe and leads to more positive emotions. In fact, being near flowers makes you three times more likely to be happy, and being in sunlight elevates mood and reduces stress. So literally stop and smell the roses. Stretch every good moment like taffy.

JUDGE NOTHING

You'll be happy

FORGIVE EVERYTHING

You'll be happier

LOVE EVERYTHING

You'll be happiest

If it doesn't bring you *inspiration* *energy* or *orgasm* it doesn't belong in your *life*

—UNKNOWN

STOP SHRINKING TO FIT INTO PLACES YOU'VE OUTGROWN.

—STEVE MARIBOLI

YOU DON'T HAVE TO MOVE MOUNTAINS.

simply fall in love with life.

BE A TORNADO OF HAPPINESS,
GRATITUDE AND ACCEPTANCE.
YOU WILL CHANGE THE WORLD
JUST BY BEING A WARM
KIND-HEARTED HUMAN BEING.

—ANITA KRIZZAN

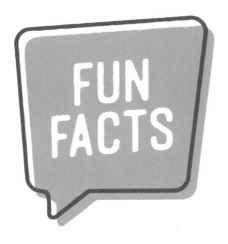

FUN FACTS

The best anti-aging strategy? Kindness. Perpetually kind people have less stress and depression and better moods and physical health, all of which lead to delayed mortality. So carry someone's groceries to the car, feed a stranger's parking meter, befriend someone who looks lonely, and expand happiness for you both.

If you're too busy to laugh,

YOU ARE TOO BUSY.

—PROVERB

A LITTLE NONSENSE, NOW AND THEN, IS RELISHED BY THE WISEST MEN.

ENJOY THE LITTLE THINGS IN LIFE FOR ONE DAY YOU MAY LOOK BACK AND REALIZE THEY WERE THE BIG THINGS

—ROBERT BRAULT

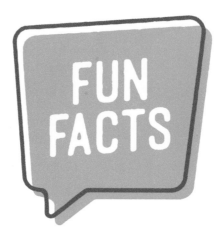

Watching videos of puppies playing or babies cooing will boost your immune system, relax your muscles, and even burn calories. What's your go-to hilarious video?

Just One of Those Days

—MICHAEL JORDAN

WE SPEND
SO MUCH TIME
being afraid of failure,
AFRAID OF REJECTION.
BUT REGRET
is the thing
WE SHOULD FEAR MOST.

—TREVOR NOAH

BRAVE DOESN'T MEAN YOU'RE NOT SCARED. IT MEANS YOU GO ON EVEN THOUGH YOU'RE SCARED.

—ANGIE THOMAS

We don't make MISTAKES; we just have HAPPY LITTLE ACCIDENTS

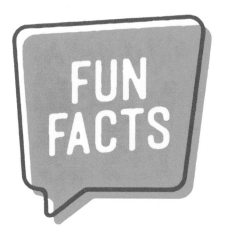

Even J.K. Rowling was rejected 12 times before a publisher signed Harry Potter, so let yourself fail. Adopt a growth mindset, find a golden nugget of wisdom and learning, read inspiring stories to regain hope, focus on your strengths, and choose optimistic thinking. Then, if all else fails, know that this too shall pass, and you will get through it.

YOU are NOT *Stuck.*

EVERYTHING **EVERYTHING** everything is *Temporary*

—CHANI NICHOLAS

Our BORDeRS and our OBSTACLES can either STOP US IN OUR TRACKS or THEY CAN FORCE US TO GET creative.

—AMY PURDY

LIFE

ALWAYS OFFERS YOU · A SECOND CHANCE

IT'S CALLED

Tomorrow

ONe SMaLL crack does NOT MEAN THAT you are **BROKeN,** IT MEANS THAT you were Put TO THE TEST aND you DIDN'T FALL APaRT.

—LINDA POINDEXTER

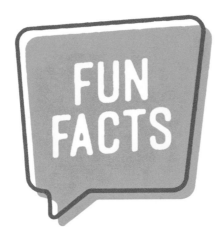

Most people know about post-traumatic stress disorder, but do you know about post-traumatic growth? When losing a loved one brings you closer to a friend, when almost dying in a car accident makes you appreciate life more, or when falling apart after job loss makes you create a new business, you grow—and we all have that capability.

I wear my MISTAKES LIKE Badges OF HONOR and CELEBRATE THEM.

—AMY SCHUMER

ONCE YOU CHOOSE Hope, ANYTHING'S POSSIBLE.

—CHRISTOPHER REEVE

WHEN WE ARE NO LONGER ABLE TO CHANGE A SITUATION, WE ARE CHALLENGED TO CHANGE OURSELVES.

—VIKTOR FRANKL

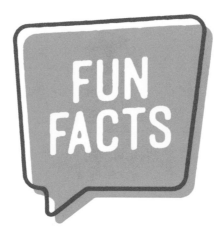

It turns out that stress isn't necessarily bad for you. What can be bad is how you view that stress. View it as harmful, and it will cause high blood pressure, inflammation, and disease. View it as a motivator and your body stays excited but calm. So pause. Breathe. And shift your mindset about stress to work for you.

YOUR *RUPTURE* IS THE ONLY WAY TO RAPTURE SAY YES TO IT ALL.

—REGENA THOMASHAUER

BROKEN CRAYONS STILL COLOR

—SHELLEY HITZ

I can be *changed* by what happens to me. BUT I REFUSE to be reduced by it.

—MAYA ANGELOU

What if Pain – like Love – is just a Place Brave People visit?

—GLENNON DOYLE

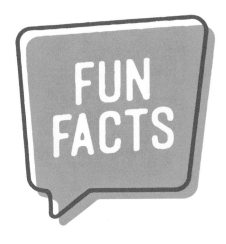

Instead of saying "I can't," ask "How can I?" Instead of "I failed," ask, "What did I learn for next time?" Research from Carol Dweck of Stanford University shows that people with a growth mindset are more resilient to challenges and more successful in the long run.

LOSERS QUIT WHEN THEY FAIL.

WINNERS

FAIL UNTIL THEY SUCCEED.

—ROBERT KIYOSAKI

YOU WILL FACE your GREATEST OPPOSITION WHEN you are CLOSEST TO your BIGGEST MIRACLE

—SHANNON L. ALDER

—UNKNOWN

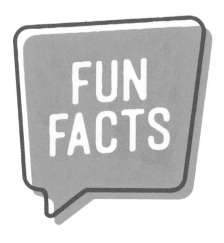

According to psychology researcher Dr. Anders Ericsson, it takes 10,000 hours of practice to become an expert at anything. Practice, practice, practice. And if you fall down during practice, get up, dust off, and keep practicing.

Step Back. Breathe. Repeat.

Wonderful You!

—CLEO WADE

YOU CAN DO HARD THINGS

(But only after you've totally freaked out about them. Once you've done that, you should be fine.)

—JON KABAT ZINN, PHD

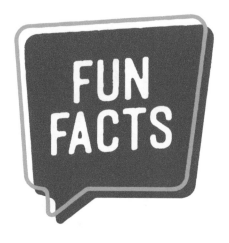

Happiness is a choice. Research conducted with twins who had been separated at birth showed that happiness comes down to the voluntary actions you choose every moment in every day. You choose how you see your day, you choose what you do with your time, you choose whether to step back and breathe—so step back and choose wisely.

Sometimes the Best Thing to do is Absolutely Nothing

—ANNE LAMOTT

SELF CARE -IS- HOW YOU TAKE YOUR POWER BACK.

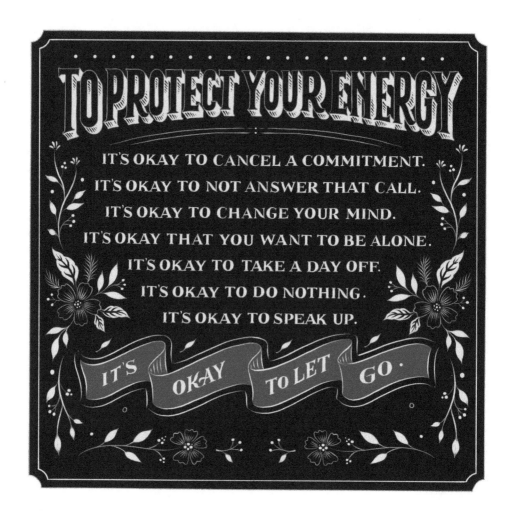

TO PROTECT YOUR ENERGY

IT'S OKAY TO CANCEL A COMMITMENT.
IT'S OKAY TO NOT ANSWER THAT CALL.
IT'S OKAY TO CHANGE YOUR MIND.
IT'S OKAY THAT YOU WANT TO BE ALONE.
IT'S OKAY TO TAKE A DAY OFF.
IT'S OKAY TO DO NOTHING.
IT'S OKAY TO SPEAK UP.

IT'S OKAY TO LET GO.

—UNKNOWN

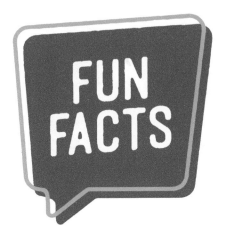

Your heart pumps 2,000 gallons of blood daily, producing enough energy to power a truck for miles. Just like a truck, your heart needs fuel in order to keep truckin' for the long haul! So slow down, pause, take a long deep breath, and recharge.

Be Nice to yourself.

IT'S HARD TO BE HAPPY
WHEN SOMEONE IS MEAN TO
YOU ALL THE TIME.

—CHRISTINE ARYLO

SeLF-Care IS GIVING the WORLD the BEST OF YOU, INSTEAD OF WHAT'S LEFT OF YOU.

—KATIE REED

LOVE yourself MORE THAN YOU LOVE YOUR DRAMA.

—JEN SINCERO

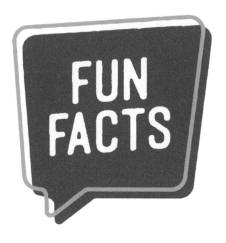

Self-care is not selfish. In fact, it's "otherish." When you're burned out, you're more temperamental, judgmental, and negative. And science shows that emotions are contagious, so filling up on self-care is the best way to change the world. Period.

FOR
FAST ACTING
RELIEF

TRY SLOWING DOWN

YOU DON'T ALWAYS NEED A PLAN.

Sometimes
you just need to

breathe,
trust,
let go
and see what
happens.

—MANDY HALE

Breathe darling

THIS IS JUST A chapter

IT'S NOT YOUR WHOLE story

—S.C. LOURIE

"Honestly, you just take a DEEP BREATH & SAY "F*CK IT""

—JOHNNY KNOXVILLE

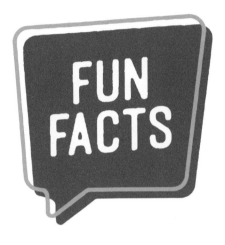

FUN FACTS

You take approximately 23,000 breaths per day, and the length and quality of your breath impacts cardiovascular health, disease, and mortality. Make those breaths count by slowing them down—inhaling for five, exhaling for five, and letting your whole body thrive.

—CHERYL STRAYED

unlike
self-criticism,
WHICH ASKS if you're
good enough,
self-compassion **ASKS**
what's good
for you?

Be Thankful For What you Have. Your Life, No matter How Bad you Think it is, is Someone else's FairyTale.

—WALE AYENI

I WAS BORN TO MAKE MISTAKES, NOT TO FAKE PERFECTION.

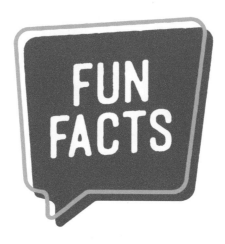

Though it seems like being hard on yourself will help you do better next time, happiness research shows that self-criticism makes you anxious, depressed, and more likely to fail again. Rather, research studies show that saying kind words and encouraging yourself will motivate you more and lead to better results. Say, "I love you," "I believe in you," or "You learned a lot and you'll get 'em next time!"

Just
for
Fun!

—UNKNOWN

"Mirror, MIRROR ON THE WALL, don't say it 'cause I KNOW I'M CUTE."

—LIZZO

SOME DAYS YOU EAT SALADS & GO TO THE GYM

SOME DAYS YOU EAT CUPCAKES & REFUSE TO PUT ON PANTS

IT'S CALLED BALANCE

—UNKNOWN

The ONLY THING Wrong WITH ME WAS THAT I THOUGHT THERE WAS Something WRONG WITH ME.

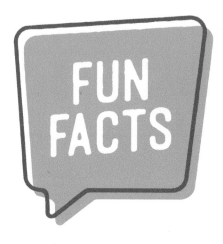

When you think about a fun, relaxing vacation or a warm, gooey cookie, you flood your brain and body with the feel-good hormone dopamine, which makes you alert, motivated, and excited. So, whether you eat the cookie or not, daydream about it and feel your happiness grow.

YOUR BODY IS NOT A TEMPLE.
IT'S AN AMUSEMENT PARK.

ENJOY -THE- RIDE.

—ANTHONY BOURDAIN

WHY *yes* I could start my day **WITHOUT COFFEE** but I like being able to remember things like how to say words & **PUT ON PANTS**

—NANEA HOFFMAN

Everybody's BORN to be different

that's the one thing that makes us THE SAME

Shut up, I think you're gorgeous.

—UNKNOWN

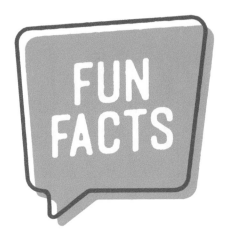

FUN FACTS

Which is easier for you to think of: What's good or what's wrong? Your talents or your weaknesses? Researchers have found that we all have something called negativity bias. To offset negativity bias, dwell on positives every day. Seek out inspiration, joy, love, gratitude—your brain will benefit!

You're ONLY GIVEN a Little SPARK OF MADNESS. You MUSTN'T Lose it.

—ROBIN WILLIAMS

Some Say
Life is Short.
I say
LIFE IS
TALL-
GRAB a
STRAW!

—SARK

Be Eccentric now.

DONT WAIT FOR OLD AGE TO WEAR PURPLE.

—REGINA BRETT

Those people who think they know everything are a great annoyance to those of us who do.

—ISAAC ASIMOV

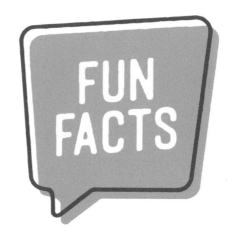

According to Gallup, the chances that another person has your exact same strengths is approximately 1 in 33 million. In other words, no one is like you, so be your wild, wacky, perfectly unique self.

HATERS ARE MY FAVORITE.

I'VE

BUILT AN EMPIRE WITH

THE BRICKS THEY'VE THROWN AT ME.

KEEP ON HATING.

—CM PUNK

WHEN LIFE SHUTS a DOOR, OPEN it again. it's a DOOR. THAT's HOW they WORK.

—UNKNOWN

DON'T HALF-A*S ANYTHING.

whatever you do, always USE YOUR FULL A*S

—KAREN SALMANSOHN

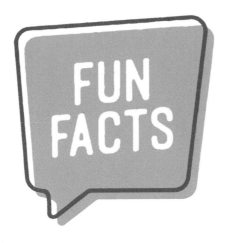

FUN
FACTS

What do you love doing for no other reason than it lights you up? Painting? Rock climbing? Singing? When an activity is so engrossing that you lose track of time, you've entered what researcher Mihaly Csikszentmihalyi, PhD, calls a state of flow—a state that's not only enjoyable but also performance enhancing.

A FACT OF LIFE: AFTER **MONDAY & TUESDAY** EVEN THE CALENDAR SAYS WTF

—UNKNOWN

We're all BRAVE in our own way. For example I am not afraid of raw cookie dough.

—UNKNOWN

Christmas is a great time BECAUSE YOU CAN SHOUT DON'T COME IN HERE! AND PEOPLE ASSUME YOU'RE WRAPPING THEIR PRESENTS, INSTEAD OF JUST WANTING TO BE LEFT ALONE.

—UNKNOWN

"I WONDERED, Why have I been chasing Happiness MY WHOLE LIFE when bliss was here ...the Entire Time?"

—ELIZABETH GILBERT

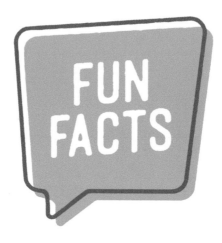

Have you ever noticed that when you're in nature, you feel happier? That's because our early ancestors lived in the wilderness, so our brains literally need nature to survive. Get outside, breathe in the air, and get your "Vitamin N" on!

Resources

Websites

Authentic Happiness: University of Pennsylvania's website for positive psychology. Take the VIA Survey of Character Strengths (free online assessment of your strengths available under the Questionnaires tab) at www.authentichappiness.com.

Live Happy Magazine: LiveHappy.com

PurposeGirls: The Women's Happiness Network Facebook Group https://www.facebook.com/groups/PurposeGirlsGroup/

Podcasts

The Flourishing Center Podcast with Emiliya Zhivotovskaya

Happier Podcast with Gretchen Rubin

The Psychology Podcast with Scott Barry Kaufman

The PurposeGirl Podcast with Carin Rockind

Books

Authentic Happiness by Dr. Martin Seligman

The Big Leap by Gay Hendricks

Big Magic by Elizabeth Gilbert

Daring Greatly by Brené Brown

Five: Where Will You Be Five Years from Today? by Gary Zadra

GRIT by Angela Duckworth

Positivity by Dr. Barbara Fredrickson

A Return to Love by Marianne Williamson

Wire Your Brain for Confidence by Louisa Jewell

You Are a Badass by Jen Sincero

Self-Compassion by Kristen Neff

Short Guide to a Happy Life by Anna Quindlen

Programs

Certificate in Applied Positive Psychology certification program via The Flourishing Center: https://theflourishingcenter.com/our-programs/certificate-in-positive-psychology-capp/

References

Alder, Shannon. 300 Questions to Ask Your Parents Before It's Too Late. Hammond, IN: Horizon, 2011.

AllGreatQuotes. "Charles M. Schulz Quotes."
https://www.allgreatquotes.com/a-little-chocolate/.

Anonymous. "If you could see yourself, just for one day, you'd see how everyone else sees you, and my God you are f*cking beautiful!" Pinterest.
https://www.pinterest.ch/pin/384002305700030591/?lp=true.

Anonymous. "Once in awhile, blow your own damn mind." Pinterest.
https://www.pinterest.com/pin/504121752035723607/?lp=true.

Awwmemes. https://awwmemes.com/i/im-not-a-princess-dont-need
-saving-i-m-a-214942bb31e9438cbe3f30ff8ebd2e14.

AZ Quotes. "Quotes › Authors › J › Janis Joplin › The more you live, the less . . ."
https://www.azquotes.com/quote/825605.

AZ Quotes. "Quotes › Authors › R › Regina Brett › Don't take yourself so seriously. No . . ." https://www.azquotes.com/quote/900034.

AZ Quotes. "Quotes › Authors › S › Sark › Some say, Life is short. I . . . ." https://www.azquotes.com/quote/1059427.

Binazir, Ali. Huffington Post. "Are You a Miracle? Probability of Your Being Born." Accessed November 11, 2019. https://www.huffpost.com/entry/probability-being-born_b_877853.

Bishop, Gary John. UNFU*K Yourself. New York: HarperOne, 2016.

Bourdain, Anthony. Kitchen Confidential: Adventures in the Culinary Underbelly, New York: Harper Collins, 2000.

Brainy Quotes. "George S. Patton Quotes." Accessed November 10, 2019. https://www.brainyquote.com/quotes/george_s_patton_161896.

Brainy Quotes. "Oprah Winfrey Quotes." Accessed November 11, 2019. https://www.brainyquote.com/quotes/oprah_winfrey_105255.

Brault, Robert. "Quotable Quotes." Readers Digest, September 1986: page 139.

Brett, Regina. "ECards," ReginaBrett.com. https://www.reginabrett.com/ecards/2015/3/29/be-eccentric-now-dont-wait-for-old-age-to-wear-purple.

Brown, Brené. Daring Greatly: How the Courage to Be Vulnerable Transforms the Way We Live, Love, Parent, and Lead. New York: Avery, 2012.

Carlson, Richard. Don't Sweat the Small Stuff, New York: Hyperion, 1997.

CBS News. "Will Smith Pursues 'Happyness.'" YouTube. December 21, 2006. https://www.youtube.com/watch?v=REo0OJJS6H4.

Chani Nicholas. "M A R S O P P O S E S S A T U R N," Facebook, June 13, 2019. https://www.facebook.com/chani.nicholas /photos/a.324727794389781/1085254361670450/?type=3&theater.

Chris_Meloni. "Don't half-ass anything. Whatever you do, always use your full ass," Twitter, October 27, 2014. https://twitter.com/chris_meloni /status/526843137659260928?lang=en.

Christakis, Nicholas A. and Fowler, James H. "Social Contagion Theory: Examining Dynamic Social Networks and Human Behavior." Statistics in Medicine. Wiley Online Library. 18 June, 2012. DOI: 10.1002/sim.5408.

Cleo Wade. "Just a friendly reminder…" Instagram, July 29, 2019. https://www.instagram.com/p/B0foO2XJbSW/.

Cole, Jordana. Personal communication with author. November 10, 2019.

CoolFunnyQuotes. "Anonymous Quote." https://www.coolfunnyquotes.com /author/anonymous/when-life-closes-a-door/.

Csikszentmihalyi, Mihaly. Flow: The Psychology of Optimal Experience. New York: Harper & Row, 1990.

Cuddy, Amy. "Your Body Language May Shape Who You Are." TED: Ideas Worth Spreading, June 2012. https://www.ted.com/talks/amy_cuddy_your_body _language_shapes_who_you_are.

Dartmouth. "Kindness Health Facts." Accessed November 11, 2019. https://www.dartmouth.edu/wellness/emotional/rakhealthfacts.pdf.

Deen, Paula. Paula Deen: It Ain't All About the Cookin'. New York: Simon and Schuster, 2009.

Diener, Ed, Frank Fujita, Louis Tay, and Robert Biswas-Diener. "Purpose, Mood, and Pleasure in Predicting Satisfaction Judgments." Social Indicators Research 105, no. 3 (2011): 333–41. https://doi.org/10.1007/s11205-011-9787-8.

Doyle, John Sean. Mud and Dreams: Essays on Falling More Deeply in Love with Life. Raleigh, NC: Rainstick Press, 2018.

Duckworth, Angela. Grit: The Power of Passion and Perseverance. New York: Simon and Schuster, 2016.

Dweck, Carol S. Mindset: The New Psychology Of Success. New York: Ballantine Books, 2008.

Ericsson, K. Anders, Ralf T. Krampe, and Clemens Tesch-Römer. "The Role of Deliberate Practice in the Acquisition of Expert Performance." Psychological Review 100, no. 3 (1993): 363–406. https://doi.org/10.1037//0033-295x.100.3.363.

Erin Van Vuren. "I will not be another flower. . . " Instagram, January 10, 2018, www.instagram.com/p/BdxtcCZlvjB/.

Flood, Allison. "JK Rowling says she received 'loads' of rejections before Harry Potter success." The Guardian. March 24, 2015. https://www.theguardian.com/books/2015/mar/24/jk-rowling-tells-fans-twitter-loads-rejections-before-harry-potter-success.

Frankl, Viktor E. Man's Search for Meaning. Boston: Beacon Press, 1959.

Fredrickson, Barbara. Positivity. New York: Crown Publishers, 2009.

Fredrickson, Fabienne. Embrace Your Magnificence: Get Out of Your Own Way and Live a Richer, Fuller, More Abundant Life. Bloomington, IN: Balboa Press, 2013.

Thef*ckitdiet. "You are not alive just to pay your bills and lose weight," Twitter, August 14, 2018, https://twitter.com/thef*ckitdiet/status/1029439637700468738?lang=en.

Genius. "Close Your Eyes." https://genius.com/Meghan-trainor-close-your-eyes-lyrics.

Gilbert, Elizabeth. Eat Pray Love. New York: Riverhead Books, 2006.

Goldman, Robert, and Stephen Papson. Nike Culture: The Sign of the Swoosh. New York: SAGE Publications Ltd., 1998.

Goodreads. "A.A. Milne > Quotes > Quotable Quote." https://www.goodreads.com/quotes/1113253-sometimes-the-smallest-things-take-up-the-most-room-in.

———. "**Arthur Ashe** > Quotes > Quotable Quote." https://www.goodreads.com/quotes/7983484-start-where-you-are-use-what-you-have-do-what.

———. "**Bernard Meltzer** > Quotes > Quotable Quote." https://www.goodreads.com/quotes/2809-a-true-friend-is-someone-who-thinks-that-you-are.

———. "**Bob Ross** > Quotes." https://www.goodreads.com/author/quotes/102372.Bob_Ross.

———. **"Bodhi Smith Impressionist Photography Quotes."** Accessed November 9, 2019. https://www.goodreads.com/work/quotes/69407270-bodhi -smith-impressionist-photography.

———. **"Caroline Myss** > Quotes > Quotable Quote." Accessed November 10, 2019. https://www.goodreads.com/quotes/464294-the-soul-always-knows -what-to-do-to-heal-itself.

———. **"Cathy Guisewite** > Quotes > Quotable Quote." https://www.goodreads .com/quotes/58237-when-life-gives-you-lemons-squirt-someone-in-the-eye.

———. **"Christine Arylo** > Quotes > Quotable Quotes." Accessed November 10, 2019. https://www.goodreads.com/author/quotes/2753080.Christine_Arylo.

———. **"Christopher Reeve** > Quotes > Quotable Quote." https://www .goodreads.com/quotes/263437-once-you-choose-hope-anything-s-possible.

———. **"CM Punk** > Quotes > Quotable Quote." https://www.goodreads.com /quotes/683637-haters-are-my-favorite-i-ve-built-an-empire-with-the.

———. **"Dolly Parton** > Quotes > Quotable Quote." https://www.goodreads.com /quotes/21268-find-out-who-you-are-and-do-it-on-purpose.

———. **"Drake** > Quotes > Quotable Quote." https://www.goodreads.com /quotes/643777-i-was-born-to-make-mistakes-not-to-fake-perfection.

———. "**Guillaume Apollinaire** > Quotes > Quotable Quote." https://www
.goodreads.com/quotes/24892-now-and-then-it-s-good-to-pause-in-our-pursuit.

———. "**Jessica Ainscough** > Quotes > Quotable Quote." https://www
.goodreads.com/quotes/6766401-don-t-let-someone-dim-your-light
-simply-because-it-s-shining.

———. "**Lalah Delia** > Quotes > Quotable Quote." Accessed November 10, 2019.
https://www.goodreads.com/quotes/8645113-self-care-is-how-you-take
-your-power-back.

———. "**Leo Buscaglia** > Quotes > Quotable Quote." https://www.goodreads
.com/quotes/84706-a-single-rose-can-be-my-garden-a-single-friend.

———. "**Mae West** > Quotes > Quotable Quote." https://www.goodreads.com
/quotes/1598-you-only-live-once-but-if-you-do-it-right.

———. "**Mallory hopkins** > Quotes > Quotable Quote." https://www.goodreads
.com/quotes/644970-life-is-short-smile-while-you-still-have-teeth.

———. "**Mary Tyler Moore** > Quotes > Quotable Quote." Accessed November
10, 2019. https://www.goodreads.com/quotes/41752-you-can-t-be-brave-if-
you-ve-only-had-wonderful-things.

———. **"Morgan Freeman Quotes."** Brainy Quotes. Accessed November 10,
2019. https://www.brainyquote.com/quotes/morgan_freeman_378380.

———. **"Rita Mae Brown** > Quotes > Quotable Quote." https://www.goodreads .com/quotes/98041-i-finally-figured-out-the-only-reason-to-be-alive.

———. **"Shirley Chisholm** > Quotes > Quotable Quote." Accessed November 8, 2019. https://www.goodreads.com/quotes/7687067-if-they-don-t-give -you-a-seat-at-the-table.

———. **"Sri Chinmoy** > Quotes > Quotable Quote." https://www.goodreads.com /quotes/223406-judge-nothing-you-will-be-happy-forgive-everything-you-will.

———. **"Steve Maraboli** > Quotes > Quotable Quote." https://www.goodreads .com/quotes/123462-happiness-is-not-the-absence-of-problems-it-s-the-ability.

Grant, Adam. Originals: How Non-Conformists Move the World. New York: Penguin Books, 2017.

Hale, Mandy. Beautiful Uncertainty. Nashville, TN: Thomas Nelson Publishing, 2016.

Hanh, Thich Nhat. Peace Is Every Step. New York: Bantam Books, 1991.

HeartMath Institute. "Heart-Focused Breathing." Accessed November 11, 2019. https://www.heartmath.org/articles-of-the-heart/the-math-of-heartmath /heart-focused-breathing/.

HelpGuide. "Laughter is the Best Medicine." Accessed November 11, 2019. https://www.helpguide.org/home-pages/emotional-intelligence.htm.

Hitz, Shelley. Broken crayons still color: From Our Mess To God's Masterpiece. Colorado Springs, CO: Body & Soul Publishing, 2016.

Hoffman, Nanea. Sweatpants & Coffee (blog). Accessed November 11, 2019. https://i.pinimg.com/originals/f7/f8/47/f7f847918fa8d-1405de0d32507688b1e.jpg.

iFunny. https://ifunny.co/picture/a-fact-of-life-after-monday -and-tuesday-even-the-XXpDyA0U5.

Imgur. "Yummy." https://imgur.com/gallery/KaknbVE.

The Irish Times. "Robin Williams: Memorable Quotes from Life and Film." The Irish Times, August 12, 2014. https://www.irishtimes.com/culture/film /robin-williams-memorable-quotes-from-life-and-film-1.1894547.

Jacobowski, Ludwig. "Leuchtende Tage." Das Magazin für Litteratur, August 1899.

Jewell, Louisa. Wire Your Brain for Confidence. The Science of Conquering Self-Doubt. Toronto: Famous Warrior Press, 2017.

Juma, Norbert. "50 Coffee Quotes to Wake You Up Every Morning." Everyday Power October 9, 2019. https://everydaypower.com/coffee-quotes/.

Junglep*ssy "Bling Bling." YouTube. June 10, 2014. https://www.youtube.com /watch?v=9MJ5RTYcfto.

Kabat-Zinn, Jon. Wherever You Go, There You Are: Mindfulness Meditation For Everyday Life. London: Hachette UK, 2016.

Karbo, Karen. The Gospel According to Coco Chanel: Life Lessons From The World's Most Elegant Woman. Guilford, CT: Morris Publishing Group, LLC, 2009.

Karen Salmansohn. "Breathe in the Good Sh*t..." Pinterest. https://www.pinterest.com/pin/117656608990552888/?lp=true.

Karen Salmansohn. "Sometimes the best thing to do is absolutely nothing. Just sit. Breathe. Be alone with your thoughts. Allow new insights to surface." Facebook. July 29, 2018. https://www.facebook.com/Notsalmon /posts/10156626614888707?comment_tracking=%7B"tn"%3A"O"%7D.

Kiyosaki, Robert. Rich Dad, Poor Dad. Scottsdale, AZ: Plata Publishing, 1997.

Knoxville, Johnny. "Johnny Knoxville here, AMA." Reddit, October 25, 2013. https://www.reddit.com/r/IAmA/comments/1p7kym/johnny_knoxville _here_ama/.

Lalah Delia. "Relax. You are still growing," Twitter. July 29, 2019. https://twitter .com/LalahDelia/status/1156033952789831,682.

Lamott, Anne. "12 Truths I Learned from Life and Writing," TED: Ideas Worth Spreading, April 2017, https://www.ted.com/talks/anne_lamott_12_truths_i _learned_from_life_and_writing?language=en.

Lee, Kevan. "Your Brain on Dopamine: The Science of Motivation." I Done This Blog. The Science of Small Wins. Accessed November 11, 2019. http://blog .idonethis.com/the-science-of-motivation-your-brain-on-dopamine/.

Lehnardt, Karin. "41 Interesting Facts About The Human Heart." Heart Check. November 28, 2016. https://www.athletictestingsolutions.com/41-interesting -facts-about-the-human-heart/.

Louv, Richard. Vitamin N: The Essential Guide to a Nature-Rich Life. Chapel Hill, NC: Algonquin Books of Chapel Hill, 2016.

Mantra Magazine. "Don't take it out on your hair. . ." Instagram, February 26, 2019. https://www.instagram.com/p/BuXdLl8BxgF/.

McGonigal, Kelly. "How to Make Stress Your Friend." TED: Ideas Worth Spread-ing, June 2013. https://www.ted.com/talks/kelly_mcgonigal_how_to _make_stress_your_friend?language=en.

McIntosh, Allyson. "21 Quotes All 20-Somethings Need to Read." Odyssey. https://www.theodysseyonline.com/21-quotes-twentysomethings-need-to-read.

Melton, Glennon Doyle. Love Warrior: A Memoir. New York: Flatiron Books, 2016.

MEME. https://me.me/i/christmas-time-is-great-because-you-can-shout dont-come-de3af595c4e84ec2a023bba40427df1c.

MetroLyrics. "Lizzo — Juice Lyrics." https://www.metrolyrics.com/juice-lyrics -lizzo.html.

The Minds Journal. "When I realized, I deserved so much better." https://themindsjournal.com/when-i-realized-i-deserved-so-much-better/.

Mindy Kaling. ""Why the f*ck not me?" should be your motto," Twitter, June 8, 2014. https://twitter.com/mindykaling/status/475515607698243584?lang=en.

Needham, Alex. "Leonard Cohen Shows There's Life in the Old Dog Yet with Launch of New Album." The Guardian, January 19, 2012. www.theguardian.com /music/2012/jan/19/leonard-cohen-old-ideas-new-album.

Neff, Kristin. Self-Compassion, New York: William Morrow, 2011.

Nelson, Alex. "30 of the Most Perfect RuPaul's Drag Race Quotes, Catch-phrases and One-liners of All Time," iNews, October 3, 2019. https://inews

.co.uk/culture/television/rupauls-drag-race-best-quotes-catchphrases
-jokes-uk-series-639275.

Niemiec, Ryan. "Research Points to Two Main Reasons to Focus on Your Strengths." VIA Institute on Character. Accessed November 11, 2019. https://www.viacharacter.org/topics/articles/research-points-two-main-reasons-focus-strengths.

Nietzsche, Friedrich. Thus Spoke Zarathustra. Ernst Schmeitzner, 1891.

Noah, Trevor. Born a Crime: Stories from a South African Childhood. New York: Spiegel & Grau, 2016.

Northwestern Medicine. "5 Benefits of Healthy Relationships." Accessed November 11, 2019. https://www.nm.org/healthbeat/healthy-tips/5-benefits-of-healthy-relationships.

Picpanzee. "If it doesn't bring you energy, inspiration or orgasm, it doesn't belong in your life." Accessed November 22, 2019. http://picpanzee.com/tag/eszterszaskin.

Poehler, Amy. Yes, Please. New York: HarperCollins, 2014.

Purdy, Amy. "Living Beyond Limits." TED: Ideas worth spreading, May 2011. https://www.ted.com/talks/amy_purdy_living_beyond_limits?language=en.

Quindlen, Anna. "A Short Guide to a Happy Life." New York: Random House, 2000.

QuoteFancy. https://quotefancy.com/quote/837315/Janis-Joplin-The-more -you-live-the-less-you-die.

Rachel Hollis. "OF course you changed . . . ," Facebook, September 5, 2019. https://www.facebook.com/TheChicSite /photos/a.199476321258/10157285793646259/?type=3&theater.

Rath, Tom. StrengthsFinder 2.0. New York: Gallup Press, 2007.

Richard Branson. "If you don't have time for the small things, you won't have time for the big things," Twitter, July 31, 2013. https://twitter.com/richardbranson /status/362528596767674368?lang=en.

Salmansohn, Karen. "Remember: If someone's trying to pull you down that means they're already beneath you," Goodreads, February 27, 2020. https:// www.goodreads.com/quotes/6893555-remember-if-someone-s-trying- to-pull-you-down-that-means.

Salters, J.N. "35 Maya Angelou Quotes That Changed My Life." The Huffington Post. May 29, 2014. https://www.huffpost.com/entry/35-maya-angelou-quotes -th_b_5412166.

Schumer, Amy. The Girl with the Lower Back Tattoo. New York: Gallery Books, 2016.

Sincero, Jen. You Are a Badass. Philadelphia, PA: Running Press, 2013.

SomeECards. "Birthday Memes." https://www.someecards.com/usercards /viewcard/MjAxMi1jZWl0NDQ1OGQ5NDZkOWJk/.

SomeECards. "Cry For Help Memes." https://www.someecards.com /usercards/viewcard/if-i-manage-to-survive-the-rest-of-the-week-i-would -like-my-straight-jacket-in-hot-pink-and-my-helmet-to-sparkle-1f452/?tag Slug=cry-for-help.

SomeECards. "Flirting Memes." https://www.someecards.com/usercards /viewcard/MjAxMi1hZjhhM2QzNjY1ZDFlZTNl/?tagSlug=flirting.

SophiaBush. "You are allowed to be both a masterpiece and a work in prog- ress, simultaneously," Twitter, November 2, 2015. https://twitter.com /sophiabush/status/661248363757764608?lang=en.

Sparks, Nicholas. The Notebook, New York: Time Warner Book Group, 1996.

Strahan, Michael. Wake Up Happy. New York: Simon and Schuster, 2015.

Strayed, Cheryl. Tiny Beautiful Things: Advice on Love and Life from Dear Sugar. New York: Vintage, 2012.

Street, Picabo. What I Know Now: Letters to My Younger Self. New York: Penguin Random House, 2006.

Team Scary Mommy. "100+ Funny Friend Jokes That Will Strengthen Your Bond," Scary Mommy. https://www.scarymommy.com/friend-jokes/.

Tedeschi, Richard G. and Lawrence G. Calhoun. Trauma and transformation: Growing in the aftermath of suffering. Thousand Oaks, CA: Sage, 1995.

Tellegen, Auke, David T. Lykken, Thomas J. Bouchard, Kimerly J. Wilcox, et al. "Personality Similarity in Twins Reared Apart and Together." Journal of Personality and Social Psychology 54, no. 6 (1988): 1031–39. https://doi.org/10.1037//0022-3514.54.6.1031.

Thomas, Angela. The Hate You Give. New York: Balzer + Bray, 2017.

Thomas, Iain. I Wrote This for You, New York: Central Avenue Publishing, 2011.

Thomashauer, Regina. Pussy: A Reclamation. Carlsbad, CA: Hay House, Inc, 2018.

Tibballs, Geoff. The Mammoth Book of Zingers, Quips, and One-Liners. Philadelphia, PA: Running Press, 2004.

Tiny Buddha. "To protect your energy... It's okay to cancel a commitment. It's okay to not answer that call. It's okay to change your mind. It's okay to want to be alone. . ." Twitter, December 14, 2017. https://twitter.com/tinybuddha /status/941397578381393926?lang=en.

———. https://tinybuddha.com/wisdom-quotes/days-eat-salads-go-gym-days -eat-cupcakes-refuse-put-pants-called-balance/.

———. https://tinybuddha.com/wisdom-quotes/if-you-are-too-busy-to-laugh-you -are-too-busy/.

———. https://tinybuddha.com/wisdom-quotes/slow-down-and-everything -you-are-chasing-will-come-around-and-catch-you/.

———. https://tinybuddha.com/wisdom-quotes/the-happiest-people-dont -have-the-best-of-everything-they-just-make-the-best-of-everything-they-have/.

———. ""Breathe, darling. This is just a chapter. It's not your whole story." ~S.C. Lourie" Twitter, June 1, 2018. https://twitter.com/tinybuddha /status/1002595694568525826.

Thetruthfulword. "One small crack does not mean . . ." Instagram, June 16, 2018. https://www.instagram.com/p/BkF0eNhhfr7/.

Tyra Banks. "About Mizz Banks." Accessed November 9, 2019. https://tyra .com/about/.

Upworthy. "Be thankful for what you have. Your life, no matter how bad you think it is, is someone else's fairy tale."

Wale Ayeni. Twitter, November 27, 2013. https://twitter.com/upworthy /status/405713730228744192?lang=en.

Vena, Jocelyn. "MTV Trailblazer Emma Stone Pays Tribute to Personal Heroes." MTV, June 3, 2012. http://www.mtv.com/news/1686420/trailblazer-emma -stone-mtv-movie-awards/.

Veronica Dearly. "You can do hard things . . . " Instagram, August 4, 2019. https://www.instagram.com/p/B0vKjXPA6s9/.

Vujicic, Nick. Life Without Limits. New York: Random House, 2010.

Wilde, Oscar. An Ideal Husband, 1895.

Williamson, Marianne. A Return to Love. New York: HarperCollins. 1992.

Worthington, Revelle. "10 Life Lessons from Maya Angelou." Ebony.com. May 28, 2014: https://www.ebony.com/black-history/10-life-lessons-from -maya-angelou-302/.

Your Tango. "41 Best Girlfriend Quotes to Use for Your Instagram Captions." May 2, 2019. https://www.yourtango.com/2017307299/instagram-captions -girlfriend-quotes.

Acknowledgments

To my partner in every way, Josh: there would be no book, no PurposeGirl without you. Thank you for dedicating your life to my dreams, helping me source quotes, find the right references, correct errors, proofread, and stay up all hours during our busiest two weeks. I love you to no end!

To Mom, for always believing in me; Dad, for won-der-full play; Sandy for telling everyone about PurposeGirl; and Neil for modeling how to be BIG— thank you all.

To my Soul Sisters who believe in me 150 percent: I wouldn't be alive or publishing without you. Stacey, Allison, Stacila, Katie, Julie, Richelle, Danielle, Holly, Heather, Michelle, Patty, Jen, Monique, Carole, Pam (and Todd), my Goddesses—Shira, Allison, Kate, Michelle, Rachel, Marie, Jess, and my AWAKEN/EMBODIED Sisters, you all elevate me beyond what I could ever be alone in this world.

Emiliya, Soul Sister, thank you also for allowing me to teach CAPP so that I stay fresh in PP.

To my PurposeGirls . . . YOU INSPIRE ME. My clients and CAPPsters, you teach me more than I can ever teach you. To my PurposeGirl Podcast listeners and community members, thank you for trusting me and changing the world one woman at a time, together.

To the University of Pennsylvania MAPP community, thank you for the best education on Earth. Margaret, Sean, Jordana, thank you for the quotes. To Dr. Glassner and the Main Line Fertility team, you gave me life, and Cleveland condo team, you cleared the way so I could write this.

To the brilliant folks at Callisto—Ashley, thank you for finding me; Elizabeth, you were instantly lovely; Crystal, thank you for directing me; and to those behind the scenes, thank you! And to all of the artists: You are geniuses!

And finally, to my readers, THANK YOU for being WONDERFUL.

About the Author

Carin Rockind, MAPP, CPC, is an expert on life purpose, happiness, women's leadership, and positive psychology. A certified life coach, speaker, and teacher, she has taught thousands of women to uncover their purpose and live in joy. She is the creator of PurposeGirl, a movement to empower purpose-driven living, and the founder of Women's Global Happiness Day—the first-ever worldwide initiative to eradicate the women's depression epidemic. The initiative has held more than 175 events to empower women's happiness in 25 countries on 6 continents.

Carin shows people how to grow from trauma, turn pain into purpose, and be the creators of their own lives. She spent five years as the "Happiness Guru" on SiriusXM Stars radio and is a regular keynote speaker for Amazon, Capital One, BMW, and other companies. Carin was one of the first 250 people to receive her master's degree in applied positive psychology from the University of Pennsylvania, where she then served as an adjunct faculty member. She is currently on faculty at The Flourishing Center in New York; she is the host of the globally ranked self-help show, The PurposeGirl Podcast; and she is an Amazon best-selling author for her contribution in *Pebbles In The Pond: Wave 3.*

A runner, writer, and dancer, Carin lives near Philadelphia, Pennsylvania, with her husband, Josh, and their Labradoodle, Charlie. Find out more about Carin, her coaching programs and e-courses, podcast, and women's happiness shop at www.PurposeGirl.com.